BRIGHTON & HO

THEN AND NOW – VOLUME 1

CHRISTOPHER HORLOCK

S. B. Publications

DEDICATION

This, my third book on Brighton's history, is for my brother, Stephen Horlock and his family – Sue, Sam and James. In the summer of 1968, he and I wandered around Brighton, taking views of recent changes to the town we had grown up in. It was then, really, that all this began.

BY THE SAME AUTHOR
Brighton – The Century In Photographs Volume I
Brighton – The Century In Photographs Volume II

First published in 2001 by S B Publications
19 Grove Road, Seaford, Sussex BN25 1TP
telephone: 01323 893498
fax: 01323 893860
email: sales@sbpublications.swinternet.co.uk

ISBN 1 85770 242 5

Typeset by JEM Editorial, JEMedit@AOL.com

Printed and bound by Tansleys the Printers
19 Broad Street
Seaford
Sussex BN25 1LS
Telephone: 01323 891019

ACKNOWLEDGEMENTS

As with previous books, the majority of photographs come from my own collection, acquired from a great variety of sources over the years, but postcard collectors and historian friends have lent several others. Robert Jeeves, of the Postcard Saloon, Queen's Road, Brighton, allowed a number of his postcard copies to be used as did Peter Booth, another card collector. Several modern views are press photographs, made available by Richard Taylor and Paul Holden, both of *The Argus*.

Tom Reeves, of the Lewes firm Edward Reeves, allowed one of his rare views of Brighton to be reproduced, and he was also responsible for copying many of the old photographs for publication.

The ever-reliable Trevor Povey and Bob Elliston both helped with information for the captions, and Jacqueline Pollard proved an excellent sounding board when trying to work out the introduction.

Most of the 1950s and 1960s photographs come from a popular series first called 'Do You Know Your Old Brighton?' then, later, 'The Changing Face of Brighton,' which ran in the *Brighton and Hove Herald* for more than 800 editions from 1953. James Gray, the Brighton historian, whom I regularly visited for nearly twenty years, compiled this series and gave me many duplicate photographs from it, some of which are included in this book. His 'new' views, of the 1950s and 1960s, are now 'old' views when compared with the 2001 pictures. Nothing stands still!

SOURCES AND REFERENCES

Local newspapers were undoubtedly the best source material when compiling the captions for this book. Back numbers of the *Evening Argus*, the *Sussex Daily News*, *Brighton and Hove Gazette* and *Brighton and Hove Herald*, were all consulted to verify dates and information.

A large number of lecture notes used by James Gray were passed on to me; these proved to be invaluable for basic facts and figures.

The main books consulted were period guides (published mainly by Ward Lock); also, *A Peep Into The Past; Brighton In The Olden Time*, by John George Bishop (published by the author, 1880); *Life In Brighton*, by Clifford Musgrave (John Halliwell Publications, 1970); *Brighton Old And New*, by Antony Dale and James Gray (EP Publishing, 1976); *A Refuge From Reality*, by D Robert Elleray (Olio Books, 1989) and, of course, *The Brighton Encyclopaedia*, by Tim Carder (East Sussex County Libraries, 1990).

SPECIAL NOTE

There have been two other 'then and now' photographic books of Brighton and Hove. These are now long out of print. The format of one old, one new picture, on adjoining pages, seems the set style for this kind of book, but I have tried to reinvent the genre a little, by still having the two main 'then and now' views, but also incorporating other material, such as old prints and photographs from other times, to provide a fuller, richer picture.

It was hard work taking the 2001 'present day' photographs. What at first appeared a straightforward task soon proved to be a series of hugely irritating, hit and miss forays, with the wrong kind of weather – too bright or too dull; traffic, particularly buses or vans, blocking the view; and all manner of other distractions. Mainly, though it was realising that the lens system used for pictures from the past didn't begin to equate with the lens system on any of the cameras I used, meaning the precise matching I was hoping for sometimes didn't come off. Also, quite often, it was just plain impossible to stand where whoever took the old photographs stood, so please don't think, 'he didn't line that one up very well,' on some of the views; it wasn't for want of trying!

Distances and measurements throughout the book are given in old imperial units. I'm sure anyone desperate for the metric equivalents will be able to work them out.

CH

College Place – Baker's, the greengrocery

CONTENTS

THE GOOD, THE BAD AND THE DOWNRIGHT UGLY

In his book *Underdog Brighton*, published in 1991, Denis 'Rocky' Hill gave details of a small, but significant survey he carried out among members of Brighton Council. He asked the simple question of whether they were Brighton-born and bred (or had come to the town before they were eighteen) or were 'outsiders'.

Of the thirty-seven who replied (eleven didn't), it was found that only nine were Brightonians, the other twenty-eight were outsiders. Hill therefore concluded that non-locals unreasonably dominated control of the key features of local life. Ten years on, my guess is that the number of outsiders is much the same. It's the case, too, with non-elected council officers. Indeed, the new chief executive of Brighton and Hove Council, David Panter, who took over in the autumn of 2001, knows the city only from his student days at Sussex University and through living locally for two years. Also, he has served on no previous council.

Could lack of local knowledge be one of the reasons why so many awful planning decisions get through, such as the appalling car park building that cut King Street in half in the 1980s?

If the powers-that-be know little of the town over which they preside – its origins and history, its development over the years, how businesses have originated, what's given the place its special feel and atmosphere – how can they make rational decisions about its future and well-being?

Actually, knocking down buildings isn't quite as easy as most people believe and often the finger of blame can't be pointed at the council at all, however much we'd like to do it.

But, as I have argued in my previous books, the worry is not only with buildings being knocked down, but the mediocrity and sameness of those that replace them. New housing recently put up in Edward Street looks exactly like new housing recently built in Worthing, which looks exactly like new housing built everywhere else. The Asda store at Hollingbury looks like most Asda stores throughout the country. Nearly all petrol stations are churned out to the same design, as are multi-screen cinema complexes, sports centres and buildings for leisure and recreation. Even modern churches have a box-like quality. Worst is the design of modern housing, which has been reduced to the architectural trickery of erecting the smallest rectangle of bricks and mortar that can be got away with, but giving the illusion these properties are much bigger and 'roomier' than they appear. Never mind the quality of these houses – and never mind the width, either! I wonder what the average room size is for houses built today, compared with those built, say, in the 1930s. The answer would probably be pretty shocking. Like everything else, it all comes down to money.

John Betjeman summed all this up in an outburst during a radio discussion of May 1953. This was actually about railway architecture and the quote is his response to how railways had an obligation to pay their way: 'To hell with obligations,' he said. 'Beauty is what matters; civilization is beauty, created architecture, the engineering of man. We'll only be remembered by our monuments, not by our blasted attempts to save money!'

Yes, it's about matters of attractiveness and heritage too, and there's the very difficult-to-answer question of whose buildings are they anyway? Isn't there enormous arrogance on the part of developers and those who destroy buildings from the past, in believing that they are actually theirs, to do with as they like?

What it all boils down to though, the very bottom line, is does it matter? Does it really matter if most contemporary buildings come out the same and eventually all old, 'one-off' buildings are lost? Should we be too bothered if another redundant theatre comes down, or another Victorian church is lost, or a further King Street car park is thrown together somewhere else in the city? Is it really so awful if new houses are tight little boxes all resembling each other? Or when, in the Hove Homebase store, we actually lose our bearings for a moment or two, and think we're in the one at Shoreham, or worse, completely lose track of where we are?

The answer is yes, yes and yes again. We should be more than bothered, we should be deeply worried about the roll-on effect of mediocre development proliferating in any town or city, but even more so in an historic place like Brighton and Hove.

'We shape our buildings, thereafter they shape us,' is a little-known

King Street as it used to look before redevelopment

Churchill quote. In other words, the architectural face of a town or city has a deep effect on the people who have to live with it. Buildings are catalysts. They affect us. They form attitudes. If they go on being increasingly bland and uniform, so too will our response to them. We won't be bothered at all by how they change. Anyone will be able to put up anything they like.

Then the rot will really set in. For if we stop responding to something so profoundly important as our everyday surroundings and our interaction with what is built, if we become uncritical of whatever money-minded developers decide to do – all thinking about the sameness in the same kind of way – we will have lost the whole orientation of how our city has come to be the way it is. And worse, we'll forget how its people have come to be the way they are too.

Buildings of the past reveal something of what we all once were.

Look at the 'now' pages that follow. We have built a better city – haven't we ?

King Street after the NCP car park was built

Christopher Horlock
September 2001

THE CHAIN PIER

Many people wonder exactly where Brighton's first pier – the Chain Pier - stood. Seen here about 1890, it went out from below New Steine, well to the east of the Old Town area, and was built originally, not as a pleasure pier, but as an embarkation jetty for ships taking passengers and goods to and from the continent. A very haphazard arrangement operated before this, with ships anchoring in deep water some distance from the shore, people and commodities transferring to them in small boats, on rafts, or even, in the case of passengers, on the backs of fishermen!

The pier was designed by Captain Samuel Brown and work started in 1822; it opened the following year. Later it became something of a pleasure pier – a place to stroll, to buy a souvenir or two and listen to a band playing on the pier head. Queen Victoria used the pier several times when returning from France and Belgium, but the arrival of the railway at Newhaven in the 1840s saw the pier slowly decline in use. In 1896, it was destroyed by a tremendous storm and the site today, seen below, is near where the terminus building for Volk's Railway presently stands on Madeira Drive.

MARINE PARADE – BRIGHTON'S THREE PIERS

This startling view, showing all three of Brighton's piers, dates from about 1892. The Chain Pier was owned by the Brighton Marine Palace and Pier Company at this time and the idea was to replace the ailing Chain Pier with the Palace Pier (but on a different site, further west), keeping the old pier open as long as possible to generate revenue.

Nature cleared the pier long before the Palace Pier was ready and the wreckage caused a huge amount of damage along the seafront, including part of the West Pier and both Volk's Electric Railway and his seashore tramroad to Rottingdean. Compensation claims prevented work on the Palace Pier progressing. The project was close to being abandoned, but due to

the intervention of engineer and philanthropist John Howard (quite a story in itself), work began again and the Palace Pier opened in 1899.

The modern view shows the Brighton Pier (as it's now called), with the derelict West Pier of 1866 still just surviving in the distance.

VOLK'S ELECTRIC RAILWAY

Magnus Volk opened his pioneering electric railway on Brighton seafront in 1883. Then it just ran from opposite the Aquarium entrance (now the Sea Life Centre) to the Chain Pier. It proved a popular novelty ride and was extended in 1884 to the Banjo Groyne. This meant Volk had to lower the line, so that it ran under the pier entrance. The view on the opposite page shows a carriage climbing the 1-in-14 gradient to regain level track along Madeira Road (as it was then called).

The chains of the pier can be seen passing through Snelling's Bazaar – a novelty and souvenir shop – where they were attached to a steel plate buried fifty feet in the cliff behind. The box-like building on the roof here was a

camera obscura, where visitors could see a panoramic view of the seafront area reflected, via a lens system, on to a huge mirrored disc. One of these may be seen today operating at the Foredown Tower, Portslade. On the left, above the carriage, are the toll-booths of the pier, which were installed on the Palace Pier in the 1930s and are still there today.

The Chain Pier bazaar and its adjoining cottages survived until 1928, when they were cleared for the rebuilding of the Aquarium and addition of shops below its new terraces, seen in the 2001 view, above. Volk's Railway survives still and is the oldest electric railway in the world.

BEACH AND PALACE PIER
Strict segregation of bathers was the rule on Brighton's beaches until 1902, with men and women designated to separate beaches. Even after this, undressing and entering the water had to be from bathing machines between 8am and 8pm. Bathing machines weren't cheap to hire – 6d for the first hour for men, 9d for women then another 6d for subsequent hours, either sex. Restrictions still applied on some beaches right through to the 1930s when, instead of machines, small tents were used for changing.

The Palace Pier was designed by Richard St George Moore and stands with its theatre of 1901 in place, but with only a very small landing stage for paddle steamers to operate from. This would be extended all round the pierhead in the 1920s. The windbreak down the centre was put up in 1906 and the central Palace of Fun, originally a winter garden, opened in 1912.

In 2001, after the loss of the theatre in 1986, massive widening of the pierhead and the recent change of name, it stands over-loaded with amusements and rides but, along with the Royal Pavilion, remains a top attraction of the city.

THE WEST PIER

An early view of the West Pier, probably in the 1880s, before widening and the addition of a pierhead pavilion in 1890. Landing stages would then be added and the pavilion converted into a theatre in 1893, operating as such right up to World War Two. A central concert hall was added in 1916.

The pier had opened in 1866 and was designed by Eusebius Birch, who was also responsible for the 1872 Brighton Aquarium (now the Sea Life Centre). It was at the height of its popularity in the 1920s; in the first year of that decade, 2,074,000 people visited the pier, the highest number it ever had in one year.

The modern view, on the facing page, shows the dilapidated pier in 2001. The story of its decline, from the late 1950s to closure in 1975, is a depressing one, the result of lack of maintenance (mostly), the impact of television and the decline of Brighton as a holiday resort. Hugely

energetic campaigning to restore the pier has, so far, seemingly amounted to very little, with the cost put at £30 million just to restore it to deck level. In 2001, plans were being drawn up to place large entertainment buildings on the lower promenade, adjoining the entrance, to generate revenue and boost the restoration programme, but as the months go by and the talking goes on and on, the pier looks frailer and frailer and a major collapse seems inevitable.

17

THE LOWER PROMENADE AND WEST PIER

Another 1880s view, looking westwards, showing the lower promenade and West Pier. The men in the centre give scale to the picture and show how huge some fishing boats were at this time. The town's fishmarket was located further east on the lower promenade, opposite the end of Black Lion Street. This moved in 1960 to Circus Street, as it was considered unhygienic and out of date. Shops and amusement arcades now occupy its site.

The old photograph shows both promenades in a fairly primitive state. There are wooden railings along King's Road and just a rough gravel path below. All this would change in 1886, when King's Road was widened southwards, over brick arches (still there in 2001) and the wooden railings were replaced by cast iron ones. A proper walkway then lined the lower promenade.

In the modern view, no fishing boats can be seen, the West Pier is derelict and stands with a large section removed. A 1930s paddling pool awaits clearance near the pier entrance, part of a comprehensive scheme to upgrade the lower promenade, which began in the 1990s. The new games court, to the left, was part of this scheme.

KING'S ROAD AND GRAND HOTEL

Between the piers stands the Grand Hotel, which opened in 1864. This view, on the opposite page, probably taken in the late 1880s, shows it as originally built by architect J H Whichcord. Then, it was the tallest building in the town and was one of the first provincial hotels to have both lifts and electric lighting. The enormous Hotel Metropole, seen in the smaller view, below, would subsequently dwarf it, going up in 1889-90. Massively assertive and built in red brick by the brilliant Victorian architect Alfred Waterhouse, the Metropole was ruined in 1960 when its central spire was removed and the rooftop altered to accommodate flats, more bedrooms and a restaurant.

Property on the right of the main view would come down in the early 1960s (as far as West Street) and the Brighton Centre of 1977 now occupies the site. The kerbside railings, in the foreground of the old view, once ran all the way from the Hove border to Kemp Town, mainly to stop horse traffic mounting the pavement. They were removed in sections, the last going in the 1920s, although exact replicas have recently been installed, to good effect, between the piers.

The Grand Hotel would be rebuilt and extended following the IRA terrorist bombing of 1984. The 2001 view shows how it lost its basic symmetry, but the extension was superbly realised, with the inspired addition of a turret at the Cannon Place corner.

KING'S ROAD

Left, one of those wonderfully animated views of Brighton that really capture the atmosphere of the place at the turn of the nineteenth century. You can almost hear the clip-clop of the horses pulling the carriages and the sound of gulls and surf breaking on the beach. Note the window cleaner in the centre and the two tradesmen with carts talking on the right of the picture.

What gives this old picture special appeal is that it's all so recognisable. The modern view of 2001 show that most of the buildings still stand, although some are dilapidated. The exception is the block in the middle distance – hotels at the time of the old view – but today the site of the Ramada Renaissance Hotel opened in 1983 (presently the Thistle).

KING'S ROAD, BRILL'S BATHS

King's Road again, this time where it meets East Street, which is behind the bath building. The date is the late 1860s. Brill's Baths, was one of a number of bathing establishments in Brighton opened to cater for residents and visitors who wished to swim or take medicinal or sea-water baths when the weather was bad, or the sea rough. Note all the chimneys – the hot baths would need huge amounts of coal to fire up the heating system. The photograph on the facing page was taken because the baths were about to come down and a new, much larger Brill's Baths open at the end of East Street, backing on to Pool Valley (originally Pool Lane). This is just glimpsed, nearing completion, in the gap between the buildings and is seen on the next double page.

However, it's an earlier bath building on this site that is the stuff of Brighton legend. This was Mahomed's Baths, seen in the old print,

which began in 1786. This building actually overlooked the sea; the road to the south – originally Grand Junction Parade – wasn't opened until 1829. Sake Dene Mahomed (inset) came from Patna, and was first (it is said) to offer Turkish baths anywhere in Britain. He also performed shampooing, which then meant a vigorous massage. The 'patient' wore a kind of flannel tent, with tuberous internal sleeves, whereby the masseur could reach in and get to the part (or parts) needing massage! He became 'Shampooing Surgeon' to George VI, at the Royal Pavilion, and his successor, William VI. Sake Dene died in 1851, aged 102, and was buried in St Nicholas's churchyard, Dyke Road. His baths were replaced by Markwell's Hotel in 1870, today the Queen's.

EAST STREET, BRILL'S BATHS

This is the bath building that replaced the one seen on the previous page, but on its new site at the southern end of East Street.

The gothic, red-brick Brill's Baths was built at a cost of £80,000. It would have been a much larger and grander building had funds permitted. The architect was George Gilbert Scott, who also designed the hotel part of St Pancras Station – the roof-line arches are very similar. The baths in turn came down in 1929 (the rear of the building in Pool Valley is seen at this time), when most bathing establishments were in

decline, and the Savoy Cinema, of 1930, replaced it. This can be seen in the 1960s view, above, but closed in 2000 and was redeveloped as offices, restaurants and a casino the following year (present-day view, right).

EAST STREET – THE WHITE HORSE HOTEL

Fortunately, someone took this photograph (facing page) of the hotel that was knocked down for the East Street Brill's Baths, seen on the previous page. This was the White Horse Hotel, seen here in 1869, or a year or so before. Pool Valley would be on the left. Built in the 1790s (probably), the hotel was one of the principal hostelries east of the Old Town area and was also used for meetings, inquests and as a base for the old county council elections.

It was also where the very first meeting of Sussex Masons took place, in 1789.

Originally the hotel was just the low building on the left; the tall property to the right was added in 1825. The hotel was demolished in 1869 and Brill's Baths rose rapidly on the site.

The 1990s view, above, shows the cinema that replaced the baths, and the modern 2001 view has this being redeveloped as the office, restaurant and casino building.

BARTHOLOMEWS – THE TOWN HALL

A view of Brighton's Town Hall, sometime about 1906, with the building almost lost amid the carts and boxes of traders from Market Street (the market is the low building, with the rounded pediment, in the background) who have virtually taken over the entire area. The Town Hall was built between 1830 and 1831. When it was completed, George IV had just died and the rail-line to Brighton was still a decade away. The small view on facing page, looking south-east, dates from about 1880, and shows

the Town Hall as originally built. Probably it was taken late in the afternoon on a Sunday, judging by the contrasting lack of market activity.

Bartholomews, where the Town Hall stands, takes its name from a priory building, named after St Bartholomew, which existed here in medieval times; it was partly destroyed during a French raid on the town in 1514 and the ruins remained until the 1590s.

The architect of the Town Hall was Thomas Cooper, who designed it in the form of a Greek Cross, but wrangles over land prevented the long, southern section being built. In 1899, extra sections in the angles of the wings were added, enlarging the building, but these have had the unfortunate effect of making it seem a rather heavy and ponderous design, when originally it was not.

Cooper also designed the original Bedford Hotel on the seafront, which was lost in a fire and rebuilt in the 1960s.

There have been many, many attempts

to demolish the Town Hall over the years, as its rooms gradually proved inadequate for the various departments it had to accommodate. It's still there today, as the 2001 view, above, shows, but largely surrounded by the modern civic centre, built adjoining the Ramada Hotel. The tall building in the background, right, is not the one in the 1906 view, but a rebuilt, 1980s version of it.

MARKET STREET – THE MARKET

The old view here was taken in Market Street, where all manner of market buildings stood over the years – hence its name. This one, which had opened in 1830, stood directly opposite the Town Hall (shadows of its pillars are cast in the centre, under the two open windows) and survived until 1900, when it was replaced straight away by another, more modern building, seen in the 1950s view. This was built in red brick and housed two long bays for fruit and vegetable sales and another, called the

Floral Hall, for flowers and fancy goods.

By the 1930s, traffic in Market Street had become too congested, and it was thought market premises were inappropriate near the town's administrative centre. In 1939 about a third of the market was removed. The interior of what remained was largely gutted and the building subsequently served as a car park.

The 1950s view, above, shows this, with the rate office occupying part of what was the northern-most bay. The 1937 market, currently in Circus Street, was the replacement building.

A new headquarters for Brighton's CID was built in the 1960s to the south of what was left of the market, but the whole site was redeveloped for the Ramada Hotel and civic centre, which at last gave the council new, purpose-built offices. The modern view, of 2001, shows the site partly occupied by the city's tourist information centre, in what is now Bartholomew Square.

MARKET STREET SHOPS

The old photograph, left, is supposedly the oldest we have of a Brighton shop, taken about 1850. It stood on the western side of Market Street, numbered 42-43, just round the corner from Nile Street (off to the left). A Mrs Elizabeth Collier has combined the two trades of stationer and ironmonger in premises that were previously a fairly large house; brushes, a watering can and various containers can all be made out for sale.

Sometime, before the century turned, the old shop was rebuilt and the 1950s view, above, right, shows this occupied by another stationery firm, Walter Gillett, which was also a printing business.

All this changed again between 1987 and 1989, when Nile Pavilions, presently on the site, went up – a stylish building, but seen as entirely out of keeping with the rest of The Lanes area.

Amazingly, despite all these changes, the small window, to the right, can be seen in all three views. How many people have looked out from there, over the last 150 years, and what did they see?

NILE STREET

This street is named after the Battle of the Nile, fought in 1798, but it existed before this as St Bartholomew's Lane. The view here, left, is from the 1880s, when cottages occupied most of the northern side (seen better in the smaller view). These were cleared in 1889 for commercial premises

seen on the next page in the 1950s, occupied by Walter Gillett's printing works. In their turn, these were demolished in the late 1980s to make way for an L-shaped redevelopment, known as Nile Pavilions, between Nile Street and Market Street. Early in 1989 the street was pedestrianised (modern view, facing page).

Gilletts became part of the Sussex Stationers group, which traded from a large store in East Street, formerly John Beal and Son, which became part of the group too. All the views look westwards to Prince Albert Street, which was originally called Bartholomew Street. This was built up later than most streets around it, the first section, through to Black Lion Street, in the mid-1830s. The change of name came about when Queen Victoria married Prince Albert in 1840, and the street had been extended to Ship Street.

BLACK LION STREET

This street takes its name from the Black Lion Brewery (part of which is the low, pebble-fronted building and granary tower in the centre of the old view, below), known to have existed in the 1500s. This first photograph was taken in 1883. The brewery is said to have been owned by Deryk Carver, a protestant burned at the stake at Lewes in 1555, during the persecutions instigated by Queen Mary. This is now contested and Carver is thought to have owned the Black Lion Inn, a totally different building on the other side of the street, demolished about 1815.

In 1889, Black Lion Street would be widened by the removal of Albert House (left) and some old cottages beyond (just visible). The lintel of one of these bore the date 1669, so were built just after the Fire of London.

The frontage of The Cricketers pub, on the right, dates from 1824, although the building itself is much older and the interior is extremely atmospheric. The large open doors, right, once led to a pound where stray animals were tethered.

The 1963 view (right, below) shows, at the end of the street, part of the Old Ship Hotel being rebuilt.

The cobble-fronted section

of the brewery was replaced by the taller brick building, seen in this view, about 1930.

The modern photograph shows the old brewery gone with a replica granary tower replacing the old one. The ancient street is now lined with featureless modern flats and offices, all traces of its historic brewery gone – once the oldest in the world – except for its ancient cellars.

39

MEETING HOUSE LANE

Into the Lanes area now and a view of this ancient route, which did indeed lead to a meeting house, which still exists, round a couple of corners, as the Font and Firkin pub (small view). This started way back in 1688, as a small Presbyterian chapel, the meeting house the name of the lane refers to. A plaque shows the building was rebuilt and enlarged in 1810. It is always claimed that David Livingstone, the

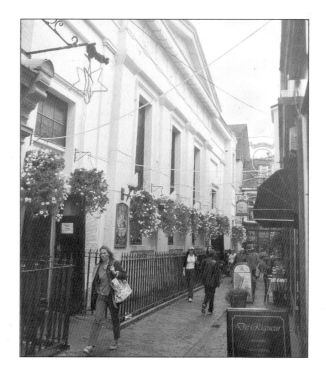

famous missionary and explorer, was married here, to Mary Moffatt, in 1845.

The view of the lane on the left of the facing page looks east, towards Brighton Place, and dates from about 1910. The top part, where the photographer was standing, is haunted by a nun who is said to pass through the wall of the Friend's Meeting House, where there is a bricked up archway.

The changes seen in the 2001 picture, right, are the result of 1960s modernisation, and The Lanes are now brimful of restaurants, fashion boutiques, antiques and fine art shops, wine bars and specialist stores.

DUKE STREET AND SHIP STREET

Another really old picture, facing page, taken about 1850. Duke Street is on the left (originally it was Craggs Lane) with Ship Street in the fore-ground where Trinity Chapel stands. This first chapel here was built in 1817 by Thomas Reade Kemp (inset, founder of Kemp Town) for a religious sect he himself devised, but one from which he distanced himself when he realised it would prevent him moving up in society circles. He sold the chapel in 1825 and it was rebuilt in the style seen, mainly in 1827.

In 1867, Duke Street would be widened by demolishing the shops and cottages on its north side (centre of the picture) leaving the chapel with no side wall. This led to the exterior being rebuilt again, in a completely different style, seen in the modern view of 2001, right. When the chapel closed in 1984 it was hoped to convert it into a museum of the history and heritage of Brighton. These plans fell through and the building at present serves a variety of on-and-off purposes, including an exhibition space.

SHIP STREET

This view, facing page, of the southern end of Ship Street was taken in the 1920s. The most significant building here is the New Ship Hotel (centre, with bow-fronted, first-floor windows) which, in its original form, can be traced back to at least 1665. The hotel was rebuilt in the early 1800s. It was this building that forced the owners of the Ship Hotel, on the other side of the street, to change the name of their premises to the Old Ship, so that people wouldn't get them muddled up. The hotel still bears this name today, of course, even though the New Ship was replaced by a Tudor-style building in 1933. Many will remember this as Henekey's restaurant and bar,

some features of which exist in the refronted premises today (2001 view).

Ship Street takes its name from the Ship Hotel, which originally fronted onto the street, but when thethoroughfare first existed and what it was originally called aren't known. There was a lot of excitement in 1961 when an old shop came down and a chimney stack was found to have the date 1713 inscribed on it, but the street existed long before this, possibly as far back as the 1500s.

MIDDLE STREET

Middle Street, another ancient thoroughfare, clearly takes its name from being located centrally in the Old Town, between East and West Streets. It is full of historic buildings, including Brighton's oldest school (founded in 1805), the finest synagogue building in all Europe and the house where William Friese-Green pioneered early colour movies.

Middle Street also has the Hippodrome theatre building still standing on its eastern side, seen in the old view opposite about 1910. This was Brighton's principal variety theatre for more than sixty years; it opened in 1901, closed in 1965 and is now a bingo hall. Middle Street School is in the distance to the left, the Friese-Green house, extreme left, with bow windows.

BOYCES STREET

The old view here, dating from about 1874, shows Boyces Street (originally Boyces Lane) looking from the West Street end towards Middle Street. The condition of the road is typical of all the streets in Brighton in the late Victorian period. None would be surfaced with tarmac until 1905. The old houses were removed in 1875 so that Middle Street School, round the corner, founded in 1805, could be rebuilt and extended. The extension is seen in the small 1950s view on the facing page.

The third view, of 1974, left on this page, shows the 1971 rebuilding of the entire school, although a tree in the corner of the playground, seen in the 1870s view, survived this. By 2001 the tree has gone, but Brighton's oldest school survives and in 2005 will be 200 years old.

WEST STREET

A view of the eastern side of West Street, dating from about 1908. Only a few of the buildings here are recognisable today; those on the left came down when the street was widened between 1925 and 1963.

Right of centre, by the flag is the Grand Concert Hall, which opened in 1867. This served many functions over the years. In the 1870s two notable lectures were given here, one by explorer and reporter Sir Henry Morton (Dr Livingstone, I presume?) Stanley and another by surgeon Frederick Treves, who is remembered for rescuing and rehabilitating John

Merrick, 'the Elephant Man'. Treves also performed the famous appendix operation on Edward VII, which delayed his coronation in 1902. The building became a skating rink in 1877, was wrecked by a gas explosion and fire in 1882 and took ten years to restore. Subsequently it became a cinema, then a restaurant, then in 1918 a cinema again, but for only a year.

The 2001 view shows how run down parts of West Street have become (middle distance), but with some sculpture recently installed, resembling giant traffic cones. Nothing seems to have become of a bold plan in the 1990s for a pedestrianised area running between West Street and East Street.

WEST STREET, THE THRALE'S HOUSE SITE

More fascinating stories of old Brighton centre around this house (small view, facing page) which was on the eastern side of West Street, where a nightclub presently stands. The house was bought in 1767 by Henry Thrale who, with his wife Hester, entertained the literary glitterati of the time, including playwright Oliver Goldsmith, diarist Fanny Burney and the grumpy Samuel Johnson, compiler of the world's first anecdotal dictionary. Note the seven posts standing outside, one of which is still in place today. It is listed, cannot be removed unless the government allows it, and probably remains the oldest piece of West Street still standing

We can still see Thrale's house in the large old photograph, which dates from 1865.

Here it's about to be demolished and replaced by the Grand Concert Hall, a building with a long, chequered history which in 1919 became Sherry's dance hall. This closed in 1948 and the building became a bingo hall, then a roller-skating rink (small view, above). It was finally demolished in 1969 when a nightclub was built on the site; the rear of the building remains in Middle Street. How that post has survived for at least 230 years is a miracle.

NORTH STREET, THE UNICORN INN

This inn stood at the top of North Street, just round the corner from Windsor Street (out of sight on the right) and could trace its origins back to 1597, when it was part of a farmhouse at the northeast extremity of the town, with fields beyond. The photograph here shows how it looked in 1892, before being rebuilt and enlarged. During demolition work, the remains of a 110ft well were unearthed, believed to be the main town well in Elizabethan times (although probably it wasn't).

The elaborate new Unicorn Inn was cleared in 1920 to create a rear entrance to the Regent Cinema, which in turn came down for the 1979 Boots building and adjoining shops, presently on the site, seen in the 2001 view.

KING STREET

The most shocking pair of photographs in the whole book. This once characterful and historic street, dating from the 1790s and named after the then reigning monarch, King George III, used to be lined with neat houses, small shops and the Running Horse pub. It ran from North Street to Church Street.

The street was somewhat run down by the 1970s, but this was seen as the opportunity to sweep virtually everything away in the 1980s for the NCP cark park building seen in the modern view. The car park cuts the street in two. It's still named King Street at the Church Street end, but is King Place on the southern side, where it meets North Street, opposite Barclays Bank.

The building is just downright ugly and its positioning represents the appalling way that money is the priority now and environmental impact is totally ignored. It is the most insensitive redevelopment ever to take place in Brighton and those council heads who thought it a good idea should be hanging in collective shame.

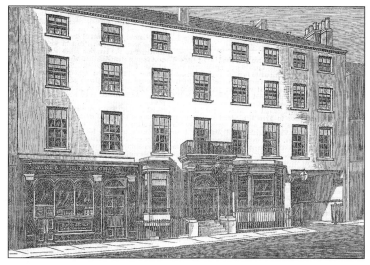

NORTH STREET

One of the oldest general views of North Street we have, fortunately showing a building that still exists. It's about 1880 and the elegant Clarence Hotel stands on the right, looking very similar to how it appears today. It opened in 1785 as the New Inn and a description of it, in 1812, details ten sitting rooms, twenty-six bedrooms, two kitchens plus music, coffee and billiard rooms. The inn's stabling could accommodate fifty horses and six coaches. It became the Clarence Hotel in 1830, the change of name coming from the new King, William IV, formerly the Duke of Clarence. The camber of the road is considerable at this time; obviously this was to take rainwater away effectively, but also the urine produced by the scores of horses that used the street every day!

The street today is dominated by traffic and the old hotel is occupied by a building society, following closure in 1972. North Street would be partly widened on its northern side during the 1870s, the 1930s and again, in other places, in the 1960s.

In 1990, when reconstruction work was taking place inside the old Hotel, it showed its age by nearly collapsing and North Street was closed to traffic for a time, below.

NEW ROAD

New Road, seen here first about 1900, was literally just that, the new road of the town, when first laid out in 1806. The Theatre Royal was one of the first buildings to appear, opening in 1807. The terrace to the left of the photograph, leading to the theatre, dates from 1820.

New Road came about through the Brighton Commissioners (forerunners of the council) agreeing to an exchange of land with the Prince of Wales. In return for shortening Great East Street (as East Street was then called), which ran straight past the Pavilion through to Church Street, thereby allowing the public easy access to his property, he gave a piece of land to the west of his grounds, along which a new road could be built. The public could then reach Church Street without peering through his windows.

The modern view of 2001 shows the bow windows of the 1820 terrace gone, which went when the colonnade was removed, in stages in 1912, 1922 and 1929. Apart from this, the view is little changed in over 100 years.

PRINCES PLACE

These four pictures show the changes to the northwest corner of Princes Place over a period of nearly 200 years. North Street is on the left in them all. The old print on the facing page is of 1807 and shows the Chapel Royal (centre), which was built between 1793 and 1795, when the town's main church, St Nicholas, had too many people wanting to attend, and a 'chapel of ease' was needed to accommodate them. The Prince of Wales, later George IV, attended this chapel (it was virtually next door to the Pavilion) but walked out when he felt a particularly critical sermon was aimed at him (and it probably was).

Next to the chapel, on the left, are two houses or shops; these are seen in the old photograph of 1879, this page, when they were about to be demolished for road widening (North Street was barely 17ft wide at this date). Removing

them left the chapel with no side wall, so it was completely rebuilt in red brick, between 1877 and 1884, to plans

drawn up by Sir Arthur Bloomfield. This started with the southern wall and addition of a clock tower. These are seen in place in the photograph, left, where the eastern wall of the chapel in Princes Place is about to come down (the colonnade has just gone) to complete the rebuilding.

The modern photograph of 2001 shows the Victorian chapel still there and still bearing the Prince of Wales's coat of arms – although out of sight here – just as the first chapel had done, despite the famous walkout.

JUBILEE STREET

Jubilee Street was named as such in 1810, when the country celebrated the Golden Jubilee of George III (father of George IV and subject of the recent film *The Madness of King George*).

The photograph here, taken about 1965, looks south, towards Church Street, with the Volunteer pub (today called the Mash Tun) in the mid-distance. Jubilee Street would close to traffic in 1977 and the shops and workshops seen here would be demolished. The street was semi-derelict at this time, the first property to be cleared went in the 1950s, the street eroding away over the next two decades, until closure. The cleared site was then used as a car park.

In 2001, after huge wrangling and any number of plans, it was finally

agreed to redevelop the site with a new library building (replacing the one in Church Street), a civic square, housing, offices, shops, a restaurant, bars and a doctor's surgery, at a cost of some £45 million.

JUBILEE STREET – SHOESMITH'S STORE

This view shows the premises of Shoesmith and Sons, corn and forage merchants, situated in a courtyard on the eastern side of Jubilee Street, not far from North Road end. The date is 1957, when much of Jubilee Street was virtually considered slum property; two years later these premises were demolished.

With hay and feed stores similar to this one, stabling, workshops and even a farmhouse, Jubilee Street must have had a particularly rustic feel to it, right up to the 1950s. When first built up it was on the northern extremity of the town, with an extensive field system surrounding it.

The corresponding

2001 view, showing the same site, was taken on the Dome car park, soon to be redeveloped as described on the previous pages. The rear of North Place forms the background.

THE ROYAL PAVILION

There have been few changes to the Royal Pavilion since it was completed in 1822 as seaside residence for George IV, but the layout of the grounds and entrances have altered over the years, particularly with the recent remodelling of the western lawns (opposite) to their original form.

The Pavilion site was first occupied by a modest farmhouse, in which the Prince of Wales took up residence in 1786. This became the Marine Pavilion in 1787 (originally Brighton House – above), designed by Henry Holland. Wings were added in 1801-02 and it was then that the Prince was presented with the famous rolls of Chinese-style wallpaper that gave him the idea for converting the original French-influenced interior to oriental. He wanted the exterior converted too, but this didn't materialise until 1813, when the Prince, now Regent and with more money to spend, had John Nash transform the Pavilion into the oriental extravaganza we see today. The cost of the conversion was more than £500,000. 'Prinny', as he was nicknamed, now King George IV, moved in during 1821, but stayed at the Pavilion only three more times before his death in 1830.

The old view of the entrance here, with the girl, dates from about 1890. The modern view shows the Pavilion looking as good as ever, still the most fantastic palace in all Europe.

THE ROYAL PAVILION – SOUTHERN GATE

These very contrasting views show the changes to the southern entrance of the Royal Pavilion and its grounds. The old print of about 1830, below, shows the original gates, which stood much further south and adjoined Castle Square. Note the sentry boxes and armed soldiers. The building on the left here is the Blue Coach Office, where Hannington's premises would later stand, at the corner of East Street.

When the Pavilion was abandoned by Queen Victoria and bought by the town in 1850, the gates seen in the print were

demolished and a new arrangement was installed two years later, seen in the old postcard view of about 1905, above. These are thought to have been designed by Richard Allen Stickney, Surveyor to the Commissioners.

In turn, these were replaced by the present gate which was unveiled in 1921 to commemorate the use of the Pavilion buildings as a military hospital for Indians in the First World War. The King, George V, had suggested this use. Indians were called on almost straight away when war had been declared as they were among the only fully-trained troops the Empire could muster then. Designed by Thomas Tyrwhitt, the

gate is seen above in the 1950s and in the centre of the 2001 view. It's generally thought to be just a bit too sombre to stand well alongside the frivolous and over-the-top Pavilion.

CASTLE SQUARE

The main picture, below, shows a vast drapery and clothing store at the corner of Castle Square and Old Steine in 1930. It was established by Robert Needham in 1848. The terrace of houses it occupied was built in 1824, just after the Royal Pavilion was completed, with the two taller houses (right) added in 1852.

Before any of this though, one of the town's most famous and opulent buildings, the Castle Hotel, occupied the site, seen in the old drawing above. This was opened in 1752 and enlarged in 1766 in response to the demand for entertainment from wealthy visitors. There they could enjoy card games, balls, concerts and opportunities for gossip and seeing who was with who. When the waltz was introduced here, in the early 1800s, it caused a sensation; a man could actually place his hand on a woman's back and half embrace her, not just hold her fingertips as in the 'up the sides and down the middle' dances of old.

The Old Ship Hotel, on the seafront, also offered similar diversions and for a while, the two co-existed. Eventually the crowds favoured the Old Ship, leading to the closure and subsequent demolition of the hotel in 1823.

Needhams closed in 1930 (the old photograph shows it boarded up) and was demolished for road widening. The replacement building is seen in the 1960s view, left, serving as showrooms for the electricity board, (opening in 1932). It became a bank building in the 1980s, seen in the 2001 picture.

OLD STEINE

The fountain in Old Steine was unveiled in May 1846, to coincide with Queen Victoria's twenty-seventh birthday. It was designed by Amon Henry Wilds and was cast at the Eagle Foundry in Gloucester Road.

The Steine is a very ancient and historic site – at first, just a large open space used by fishermen as a drying ground for their nets. The word 'steine' is of Flemish origin and means a rock or rocky place. Apparently, there used to be a ledge of chalk rocks at the southern end of the ground, subsequently giving the area its name. A stream, known as the Wellesbourne, ran through the Steine until 1793, when it was enclosed in a sewer.

With the coming of wealthy, fashionable visitors from the 1750s onwards, most seeking the sea-

water cure and other diversions, the Steine became an area for promenading and was surrounded by iron railings in 1823 and lit by gas the following year. The first proper building to go up was a library, in 1760, then fine, large houses, from 1780 (South and North Parades). This meant the fishermen had to dry their nets by draping them over the seafront railings, the start of the gradual decline of fishermen's rights in the town, ending in 1960, when they were finally forced off the seafront for good.

The old photograph dates from about 1890. Today the Steine is treated more as a park than a garden area and is something of a meeting place, particularly for students visiting the town.

ST JAMES'S STREET

Busy and bustling then as now, the middle part of St James's Street is seen, facing page, about 1910, with German Place off to the right. This was renamed Madeira Place early in the First World War when any name connected with Germany was altered.

The 2001 view shows a large 1960s store on the left, which was occupied by F W Woolworth until 1986.

The pub and shops on the right of the view are little changed and the street still has something of its original character intact, despite a certain seediness to some parts.

St James's Street was built up from about 1785. The lower part was first called Craven Buildings then, from Charles Street eastwards, Prospect Row. The present name, coming from the royal residence, St. James's Palace, was adopted in about 1803.

UPPER ST JAMES'S STREET

Huge changes have occurred further east from the previous views, making this part of Upper St James's Street unrecognisable from the animated old photograph of about 1912. This shows the northern side of the street stretching away eastwards to Bristol Road. All these shops were lost in the 1970s, when large-scale clearance took place, and the flats seen in the 2001 view were built. The southern side remains virtually intact, but the two pictures contrasted show how barren and lifeless an area can be rendered, through mediocre redevelopment.

EDWARD STREET

The old view here dates from 1937 and looks west, from the corner of George Street, down towards the Pavilion grounds. The Dome is just visible, with John Street running off to the right. The widening of Edward Street was well under way at this time, having started in 1928 at the north-east corner with Grand Parade, but the clearance is out of sight, opposite the van in the distance and concealed by the shops. The pub on the left, the Thurlow Arms, dates from about 1806, just a few years after

Edward Street had begun to be laid out, and has recently been renamed The Jury's Out, due to its proximity to the law courts on the other side of the road.

The 2001 view shows offices and law court buildings that went up on the northern side, starting in the 1960s when the road was fully widened, again creating a sterile, soulless feel to a once vibrant, bustling street.

LEICESTER STREET

Heading up Edward Street and across Egremont Place, the first street reached was Leicester Street, built some-time between 1810 and 1820, as Edward Street was extended eastwards. It is seen here, right, in 1961, prior to demolition for the widening of Edward Street – a job that had started back in 1928 at the Grand Parade end, but not reaching Park Street until the early 1970s.

At the top of Leicester Street was a gate leading to Pilgrim's Cottages, a short back-to-back terrace of eighteen charity homes, dating from 1854 and built by the wealthy Soames family for the benefit of those in

reduced circumstances over the age of sixty. In the 1950s the weekly rent was three shillings (15p today). These cottages, pictured right, were demolished late in 1968. The 2001 view is another that dismays, with modern shop premises all but blocking the street off.

KEMP TOWN BREWERY – JUNCTION OF SUTHERLAND ROAD AND EASTERN ROAD

The Kemp Town Brewery was once a large employer in the town, with its main brewing premises in Seymour Street.

The brewery began life in the 1830s, when William Hallett founded the Bristol Brewery. A series of amalgamations followed, with the firm becoming Hallett and Abbey, then Abbey and Sons and finally, in 1908, the Kemp Town Brewery. Charringtons took over in 1954 but stopped brewing in Brighton in 1964 and moved to larger and more up-to-date premises in Newhaven. All the brewery buildings came down in 1970-71, including the malthouse and storage building seen here, which was a rebuilding of a malthouse gutted in a fire of 1907. It was replaced by the Woolton building for Brighton College in 1971, an architectural non-event.

KEMP TOWN STATION

It's surprising to know that a railway once served Kemp Town. The terminus building, seen in about 1970, stood in what was then Coalbrook Road. It was an amazingly costly and difficult line to build, despite being only a mile and a quarter long, requiring a tunnel under Freshfield Road, Queen's Park Road and Elm Grove, a bridge over Hartington Road and a massive viaduct spanning Lewes Road (see page 108). Although it served the Kemp Town area, it was clearly built to block rival firms building a new line into Brighton, terminating in the Kemp Town area.

The line opened in 1869, closed to passengers in 1933, then handled goods, mostly coal, until finally closing in 1971. The site became the Freshfield Industrial Estate and the car park (small picture) of the Gala bingo hall.

ST MATTHEW'S CHURCH

This church stood in Sutherland Road, at the corner of College Terrace, and existed first as the modest chapel seen in the small picture on the facing page. The much larger stone church on the site was built in 1881-83 to designs by John Horton. Like several other Brighton churches, it was to have a tower and spire, but these were never built.

However, by the mid-1960s, the church authorities thought there were too many churches in this part of Brighton, with six all within 600 yards of each other. St Matthew's, and All Souls, in Eastern Road, were accordingly declared redundant and demolished.

St Matthew's came down in 1967 and the congregation joined St Mark's, Eastern Road. St Matthew's Court, a block of flats, was built on the site (2001 view). All Souls in Eastern Road came down in 1968.

EASTERN ROAD

One of the few pairs of pictures in the whole book where hardly any changes have taken place. This is the leafy stretch of Eastern Road between Walpole Road and Upper Abbey Road, seen from the corner of College Place, which still retains something of its period spaciousness and feel, despite the parked cars and frequent snarl-ups of traffic going to and from the Royal Sussex Hospital. Eastern Road was obviously named from its location (it's the road going east) and began to be built up as a continuation of Edward Street. The houses in the middle distance were built in the early 1900s.

The wall on the left enclosed the grounds of a girls' school, the Convent of the Blessed Sacrament, which was established in 1886 by a community of nuns from Valence in France. Ninety-one years later the school closed, the sisters removed to The Towers at Beeding, and Brighton College bought the building to house its Junior School.

THE ROYAL SUSSEX COUNTY HOSPITAL

The fascination of the old view here, dating from about 1870, is not so much seeing the Royal Sussex County Hospital all those years ago, but the absence of any other streets and houses south of it.

The Royal Sussex first opened in 1828 as The Sussex County Hospital And General Sea-Bathing Infirmary, designed by Charles Barry. It could take eighty patients and was financed by charitable subscriptions (pledged donations). It has been extended and enlarged ever since, particularly in Victorian times. The present entrance dates from 1929 and the huge tower block in Bristol Gate (out of sight here) is obviously late 1960s. More redevelopment and expansion started in the 1990s, still under way when the 2001 view was taken.

ENTRANCE TO MANOR FARM

The views here relate to what was once the most important single
building in Kemp Town – the Manor House. The entrance lodge is
seen below just before it was demolished in 1936, and Manor Road,

running north, was created. Farmland formed most of the estate, and a common sight, for many years, was to see cattle being driven through the gates of the lodge, following milking at premises in Church Place, immediately south of the entrance. The Manor House itself was off to the right and is seen in the smaller view on the facing page. It was built about 1855 for William Hallett, founder of the Kemp Town Brewery and the town's second mayor.

The Corporation bought forty-one acres of land here in 1936 and, initially, 422 houses went up – the start of the Manor Farm estate – for families displaced by the huge slum clearance scheme taking place

in the Carlton Hill, Sussex Street and Richmond Street areas. More went up after the Second World War and the Manor House survived all through the redevelopment, finally succumbing to demolition in the 1970s.

The 2001 photograph, above, shows the trees still in place, but the buildings on the right have gone, bringing into view a convent building of 1906 and its rebuilt chapel of 1994. The other view on this page is the site of the Manor House.

ROCK PLACE

This early view here, of about 1908, is dominated by the motor bus, with its registration plate CD 236. Buses like this one first appeared in Brighton either right at the end of 1903, or very early 1904, and there were soon complaints about the noise they made, the speed they travelled at and, by 1907, whether smoking should be allowed on them. Closed buses, with no open top, would not be introduced until the 1920s.

The Rock Inn and adjoining buildings have hardly changed over the years and the pub still looks in sound condition now, nearly 100 years later (note even the drainpipes and chimney pots are the same in the 2001 view – things were built to last then!). Rock Street was built up in the 1820s and is contemporary with far grander areas of Kemp Town, such as Arundel and Eastern Terraces and Lewes Crescent.

SUDELEY PLACE

Another street of the Kemp Town area; this is Sudeley Place, built in the 1860s, with Sudeley Street running off to the left. The old view dates from about 1908 and the trees seem recently planted. The unusual name for this street (and others in the area) comes from the wealthy Sudeley family, who were mostly barons, the famous one being the Sudeley who married the widowed Catherine Parr, sixth wife of Henry VIII.

Sudeley Place was originally named Mill Place, as there was once a windmill in the area. This was the East Mill, dating from the 1790s; its round mill-house and owner's cottage stood on what would now be the rear of 162 Marine Parade. This was removed, about 1845, to Sussex Street, where it was generally known as Taylor's Mill.

A row of small houses off Sudeley Place, known as Millfield Cottages, are named from the East Mill, and were built in the 1830s, while the mill still stood in the area.

THE CONTINENTALE CINEMA

This picture, right, is the most modern of the 'old' photographs in the book, dating from 1983. It shows the Continentale Cinema, standing in Sudeley Place, three years before closure and subsequent conversion into housing.

The cinema began life as a congregational chapel in the 1880s before

becoming a 300-seat cinema, the King's Cliff, in 1920. Sound was installed in 1930 and the cinema flourished despite competition from the much larger Odeon in nearby St George's Road, which opened in 1934.

In 1947 the building became a theatre, known as the Playhouse Repertory Theatre, but this venture lasted only a couple of years, the building becoming a cinema again in 1949, called the Picture Playhouse. This became the Continentale in 1951, later gaining something of a reputation for the sex films it showed. The modern view of 2001 shows the former cinema in residential use and someone's front door stands where the couple in the other photograph were going in to see *Eager Fingers, Eager Lips*.

COLLEGE PLACE – BAKER'S THE GREENGROCERY

Very little is known about this shop, at 11 College Place (next to the Wellington Hotel), belonging to greengrocer George Baker. It's just another Brighton picture of about 1890, that has somehow survived and come down to us, showing father and son (or perhaps delivery boy) in the doorway of a modest shop, decked out with the best it had to offer.

There is always huge poignancy to any view like this, where a small business and its proud owner have been caught in time by a photograph, which is now all that's left of them. We can only look into the man's face and guess what he was like, what made him laugh, what sort of life he had. It's the same, too, with any person pictured in any of the old photographs in this book.

The shop was later run by a John Baker (the son?) until the early 1950s, when it became the house it is today (2001 view). This was occupied by a Bernard Baker (almost certainly another member of the family) until the mid-1960s.

THE ROYAL GERMAN SPA

This elegant spa building opened in Brighton Park (the original name for Queen's Park) in 1825, though the old drawing opposite shows it in the early 1840s. Visitors had to pay to use the park then, the owner being Thomas Attree, who lived in a villa (the Attree Villa – demolished in 1972) at the northern end, where the surviving 'Pepper Pot' was the water tower for his estate.

Drinking spring water was fashionable among wealthy visitors at this time and while the site of the spa had no natural spring, it had a 150ft well, so the proprietor, a Dr F A Struve, had all manner of artificial blends concocted on the site, with no-one seeming to mind they weren't the genuine article.

When William IV and Queen Adelaide patronised the spa in the 1830s, the park was renamed Queen's Park, in honour of the King's wife. It would be another sixty years before the park was open to the public though (1892), when it was bought, rather strangely, by the Trustees of Brighton Race Stand, a group originally founded to upgrade the town's racecourse and establish a race fund.

The small photograph shows the spa derelict sometime in the late 1960s, when ownership had passed to Brighton Council. The firm of Hooper-Struve had vacated the building in 1963 (successors to Dr Struve's original business), having used it for bottling fizzy drinks, and a long dispute about the fate of the spa began. This was resolved with it being partly restored, as in the 2001 view, and a nursery school built, adjoining it, which opened in 1977. The open loggia of the spa now serves occasionally as a stage for productions in the Brighton Festival.

THE RED LION PUB

Three photographs showing changes to the Red Lion Pub in Upper Park Place (Queen's Park Road is off to the right). The first view, showing the original 1860s building, was taken in 1963, when virtually everything else in the area had come down (the Zylo works can just be seen on the right) and it looked like the pub might do as well. It survived and was rebuilt in 1965-1966. This version is seen in the second view, left, taken in 1985. Early in 2001, the pub was – unusually - converted into housing, seen in the modern view, above.

QUEENS PARK ROAD

The view here of about 1908 shows the length of Queen's Park Road between Albion Hill and Islingwood Road, with a tram the only vehicle in sight. Trams ran in Brighton from 1901 until 1939, when they were replaced by trolley buses. The routes were opened in stages, the one here, branching off Elm Grove and running south to Egremont Place and Rock Gardens, was one of the first to operate. The route from the station to the Steine was, surprisingly, the last, starting in 1904.

The houses forming the background in this view were built in the early 1870s (a map of 1875 shows nearly all of them in place) and the road then was called Park Road East.

ELM GROVE TRAMS

Elm Grove takes its name from the elm trees that were planted down both sides, virtually top to bottom, in 1852.

Here the view dates from 1938 and shows race day trams at the top of Elm Grove, with what is now Brighton's General Hospital hidden behind them. Originally this was Brighton's workhouse, which opened in 1867.

The tram system was so efficient, it could clear the race ground of thousands of spectators in a matter of minutes, tram after tram whisking them away, with more coming up Elm Grove until everyone had gone.

SUNDAY SCHOOL OUTING

This postcard view of a church outing dates from 1913. It shows members of the Islingwood Road Mission making their way to the top of Islingwood Road, passing Finsbury Road on their right. This is almost certainly a Sunday school outing, going to Queen's Park or the Race Hill for games and a picnic tea. They could be on their way to Kemp Town Station, to catch the train, via Brighton, for Burgess Hill, where there were pleasure gardens and a lake for boating. Such simple events would have been a big thrill for youngsters then, something they would look forward to for weeks, and would talk about for just as long afterwards. The Mission flourishes still, under the name of the Islingwood Road Evangelical Free Church; the centenary of their headquarters took place in 1999.

The modern view of 2001 is obviously very unanimated by comparison. The large house on the corner has been rebuilt and enlarged, but the roads in the area have become just more places to park cars.

SOUTHOVER STREET

Another postcard view looking west down Southover Street towards the Level. The year is about 1910. If a car had made an appearance in the road at this time it would have been a big enough event to make people come out of their shops and houses to look at it.

The cobbled wall on the extreme right is where a

boy's Annunciation School stood at this time, which had opened in 1865.

Southover Street was first built up in the 1820s, when the town was rapidly expanding and new streets were hurriedly built north-east of the Sussex Street and Albion Hill area, to house ever-increasing numbers of workers needed, now the King of England was in residence at his Pavilion and fashionable visitors had to be accommodated. Another spate of building took place in Southover Street during the 1860s.

The 2001 view shows few changes to the actual buildings, but again, character and life have been dissipated somehow. Hanover's community centre now occupies the school building and the old entrance (small view) still remains with SM above it, standing for St Mary's, the school's original name. Its old wall has been rebuilt though.

LEWES ROAD

Opposite is one of many views taken in the early 1900s to record the town's tramway system being built. It dates from 1901, when the first rails were laid along Lewes Road, up Elm Grove, then round into Queen's Park Road. The background is dominated by the church of St Martin, designed by George Somers Clarke and built in 1872-75. The second view, above, shows the scene in the 1950s, with trolleybus wires visible (trams were withdrawn in 1939) and all the trees on the eastern side of the road gone. Most of these were removed once the trams were up and running in Lewes Road, as low branches often scraped the top decks causing damage, and also, sometimes clipped passengers.

The modern view of 2001 shows Lewes Road still lined with small shops and retaining something of the lively, bustling feel of its past.

THE GAIETY CINEMA

This cinema was clearly built to serve the new housing estates going up along the Lewes Road, north of Brighton, and stood on the corner of Lewes and Hollingdean Roads. It opened in 1937, had 1,400 seats and was designed by Frederick W Morgan. Its most distinguishing feature was the 50ft, neon-lit frontage, which was described as a 'new landmark for Brighton'. The opening ceremony is seen, above with Sir Alfred Cooper Rawson, Conservative MP (in glasses, left of centre) presiding.

During the Second World War the cinema was used for showing films to troops stationed at Preston Barracks (public performances continued) and it was known as the AKC cinema (Army Kinematograph Corps). It continued as the Gaiety until 1965, when it became the Ace, and unfortunately the tower was all but removed. In 1971, the cinema became the Vogue and pornographic films were screened, coupled with live striptease shows. In 1979 it took the name of the Classic, when another cinema of that name closed in Western Road. Final closure came in 1979 and the cinema was demolished for a new road system around a new Sainsbury's store, which opened in 1985. The small view shows the cinema derelict in 1983, the 2001 picture, the site today.

107

LEWES ROAD
This 1930s view looks south, with Bear Road on the left and Hollingdean Road on the right. The Gaiety Cinema (previous pages) was built where the houses and trees are, on the right. The railway viaduct, in the distance, was part of the Kemp Town line (page 83). The strange castle-like structure, left of the arch, is the tower of the entrance building to the large

Extra-Mural Cemetery, which opened in 1857, and is now part of Woodvale cemetery.

The 2001 view is cluttered up with traffic, traffic lights and signs and the human scale of the 1930s road has been lost. The viaduct came down in sections during the 1970s and 1980s, the last part going in 1983. The cemetery tower and lodge were demolished in 1961 and replaced by a mortuary building, which opened the following year.

LEWES ROAD

NATAL AND LEWES ROADS

A really important old photograph of the Lewes Road area, looking down Natal Road about 1904. The main interest is seeing how little the area is built up and how the old Brighton-Preston boundary stands out, running down the hill on the right, across the Lewes Road, then up the hill, across fields, to Boundary House in Ditchling Road, in the very far distance. One of the small

houses in Lewes Road, to the right, was once, supposedly, a tollkeeper's cottage.

To the left is the factory occupied by the Reason Manufacturing Company, which was taken over in the 1920s by Allen West, the well-known Brighton electrical engineers, founded in 1910.

The intermediary view, below, of the 1950s, shows some of the Hollingdean estate in place, with Allen West's premises vastly enlarged. Allotments now cover some of the hill in the distance, with the old boundary line still visible.

The modern 2001 view shows the fields and allotments landscaped, the Allen West factory gone (demolished in 1972) and Sussex University's Mithras House, of 1966, standing on the left. The Air Training Corps building, one of the few remaining from Preston Barracks, can be seen left of centre. The photographs here represent how all the roads feeding into Brighton and Hove have been similarly urbanised over the last hundred years, with much being gained in the process, but much also lost.

LONDON ROAD

The old view here is of London Road (Queen's Road originally) taken a few years before the First World War. The scene is just about recognisable today, in spite of the many changes over the years.

To the left of the tram in the distance is a motor car, once a rare sight in London Road! Many well-known firms were in business at this time – Freeman Hardy and Willis (shoes), Boots (chemist), Clarkes (bakers), Sainsbury (groceries) and Corralls (coal). On the right is the Prince of Wales pub. Outside, for many, many years was a

milestone with the distance to London on it, dating from when stagecoaches travelled the London Road and none of the buildings here existed. Unfortunately, it's obscured by the passing cyclist and was probably removed in the 1920s.

The 2001 view shows some old buildings remaining, but the road now looks like everywhere else – featureless modern shops and fast-food outlets jostling uneasily with period premises – and the place seems tacky and run-down. How shops here will fare when the nearby station site is developed, with a new superstore, is a matter of huge concern for traders.

LONGHURST'S BREWERY

This view of Longhurst's Amber Ale Brewery, standing between Stanley Road and Viaduct Road, was taken by Edward Fox in 1879. The man to the left is standing in Beaconsfield Road. The name Preston Circus was not used for the road layout here, until 1906.

The brewery was built about 1840 and

originally the premises were much smaller (part of the original is in the centre, with the tall chimney), rebuilding taking place in 1881. Virtually everything came down in 1901 when the tramway system was being laid out and an easy curve to the tracks was needed at the turning into Viaduct Road.

Originally, the site was intended for the main tram terminus, but the ground wasn't stable enough to take heavy maintenance plant (due to the Wellesbourne River running under it), so it was relocated to

Lewes Road. The small picture, left, shows the brewery coming down and the 1920s photograph, below, right, has the fire station (1901) and cinema (1910) that were built on the site. The 2001 view shows today's fire station, designed by Graeme Highet, which opened in 1938. On the extreme left of the two main views is the Stanford Arms Inn, built in 1874.

OPENING OF THE DUKE OF YORK'S CINEMA
Another of Brighton and Hove's cinemas is seen here, one that fortunately still exists. The Duke of York's at Preston Circus is the city's oldest surviving cinema building, dating from 1910, and the opening ceremony has been preserved in this old photograph. The project was financed by a former actress, Violet Melnotte-Wyatt who, with her husband, had built the Duke of York's Theatre in London in 1892 (they gave their new cinema the same name). It had 800 seats and the first film shown was *Byways of Byron*, made by local film pioneer George Albert Smith, of Hove. Seats were 3d, 6d and 1/-, with boxes at 2/6d.

The lower view here shows the cinema in the 1920s.

The Duke of York's has been kept going by skilful management over the years, sometimes being run as a cinema club, where a subscription is charged. With the loss of so many cinemas in Brighton and Hove during the last forty years, the way the Duke of York's has not only survived, but prospered, is a real cause for celebration.

NEW ENGLAND STREET

The 'old' photograph here was taken in 1955 and shows New England Street a few years before the powers-that-be decided the area needed re-developing and dozens of perfectly reasonable houses were swept away in the name of progress.

The smaller view, below, shows the scene in the 1960s, with part of New

England House on the right, built in 1962. New England Street used to run to Ann Street, but today ends at Cheapside, with no houses at all along its length. It's an untidy thoroughfare now (2001 view), with nothing notable in it and another example of how redevelopment has led to sterility and dourness, in a once lively and populous area.

LONDON ROAD

Here, we have a 1904 view of London Road at Withdean, which featured in a 1976 'then and now' book on Brighton, written by Antony Dale, with photographs by James Gray. Dale thought that no two views taken at an interval of seventy years could better illustrate the changes to the pattern of life that had taken place in the twentieth century. In 1904 the horse bus still ruled s u p r e m e on the roads and no one had thought of coming to Brighton by car instead of by

train. The farmhouse of Home Farm is to the right, between the trees, with one of its barns standing across the road on the left, near where Tongdean Lane would later be sited. 'Everything has been sacrificed to king motor car,' Dale commented about the modern view. The barn went in 1960 and flats occupy the site today. The farmhouse remains (out of sight), but the 2001 picture again has a barrenness and lack of human feel that characterises most of the roads on the outskirts of Brighton and Hove.

WESTERN ROAD

Another of the city's main thorough-fares, Western Road, is seen in 1902, decorated with flags and bunting for the coronation of Edward VII, Queen Victoria's son. The location is the eastern end where, today, the Churchill Square shopping centre stands off to the left, and 1930s deco-style shops are on the right. Back in 1902 it was still possible to walk along the northern side of Western Road (right) and find a modest house, complete with front garden, in between all the shops.

The turning on the extreme left here is Upper Russell Street, a tiny part of which still exists.

The intermediary view was taken in the mid-1950s and shows the shops on the left of the 1902 picture largely intact, and the 1930s buildings, which went up when Western Road was widened.

The 2001 picture shows all the old shops to the south gone, with the second Churchill Square shopping centre (which opened in September 1998, at a cost of £90 million) in place, but out of sight.

GRENVILLE PLACE

This street was the first to be built in the Western Road area (when Western Road was just a rough track between fields to Hove), houses starting to go up from the very early 1800s. The view dates from about 1962 and looks eastwards towards the Cranbourne Arms pub at the top of Cranbourne Street. The smaller view shows some of the very attractive houses to be found on the southern side, with tarred cobble frontages and bow windows.

Grenville Place came down in two phases for the first Churchill Square development, which opened in 1968 and cost £9 million to build. The southern side (right) was cleared in 1963, the northern side, along with the shops in Western Road it backed onto, seen on the previous pages, went in 1967. The 2001 view above is dominated by the frontage of Churchill Square shops, but the pub can still be made out in the distance.

SPRING STREET

This old view, looking up the street from Western Road, almost certainly dates from 1909; the newspaper board on the left gives details of a mail van accident, which happened in August that year. Behind the two men, the Shakespeare's Head pub is taking deliveries and on the other side of the street, churns and carts belonging to A Gearing, dairyman, are assembled (one cart is coming own the hill). The cottages beyond the carts date from 1823.

In the 2001 view, most changes are to property left and right in the foreground, the result of road widening and rebuilding in the 1930s, and of course, the street is packed with cars.

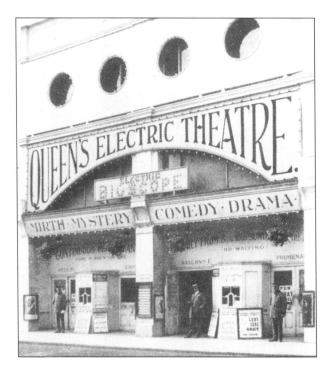

THE SCALA CINEMA

Back to Western Road itself (the northern side) and a 1920s view of the Scala Cinema, left, proudly advertising itself, standing just around the corner from Montpelier Road (off to the left). A cinema building had opened on this site much earlier, when moving pictures were the great new novelty in entertainment. The small view, above, shows these original premises - the Queen's Electric Theatre - in 1911, two years after first opening in a converted shop. It next became the Scala, from

1923 to 1932, then the Regal until 1936. For the following thirty-eight years it was the Curzon, below, then finally it became the Classic, which closed in 1979, mainly because of competition from the 1973 triple-screen Odeon at the bottom of West Street.

The modern 2001 view shows the western end of the Waitrose store that was built on the site, following closure and demolition. The mouldings on the left can be found in the 1920s view.

WESTERN HOUSE

Amon Wilds and Charles Augustus Busby, the architects responsible for much of Regency Brighton, built this extremely large house, looking part church, part castle, on the southern side of Western Road between 1822 and 1825. Its original name was Gothic House (its address was 1 Western Terrace) but later it became known as Priory Lodge. The old photograph, left, dates from the 1870s.

The house was first extended to the west by an auctioneer named Strevens, but the main changes came in 1898 when it was converted into an outfitters and milliner's premises (above) by A G Sharman. His shop frontage was extended to the south and west when taken over by Plummer Roddis in 1920. Debenhams subsequently occupied the premises, but moved in 1998 to a new store in the rebuilt Churchill Square.

The 2001 view shows the building under conversion into new shops, a restaurant and apartments, at a cost of £7.5 million.

CHURCH ROAD

Across the (old) border now, into Hove, for the final photographs in this book. The old view here, of about 1890, shows the Brighton Brewery, opened in 1851, at the junction of Church Road and what was then Osborne Street, now Osborne Villas. It dominates the picture as it dominated the area, drastically narrowing the width of the road for any vehicles passing through. This 'bunion' came down in 1902, to ease traffic flow, and the build up of vehicles has carried on, unabated, ever since.

The gasometer stands on the site of Hove's first gasworks, built in 1835 (by the Brighton and Hove General Gas Company). It ceased operating in 1870 when new works at Portslade opened. Gas was also stored on the site and the number of gasometers varied from five in 1861, to four in 1869, then six (even though the works had closed) in 1885. Today a single redundant one is left.

NEW CHURCH ROAD

Yet another example of how penny-pinching rebuilding robs an area of its individuality, style and human scale.

The large Victorian house seen in the 1960s view, built at the corner of Pembroke Avenue, came down shortly after the photograph was taken and was replaced by the very ordinary Pembroke Court flats, seen in the 2001 view. This kind of redevelopment was typical of the fate of many large houses in Brighton and Hove (virtually all the large houses along the London Road, in the Preston Park and Withdean area, have gone) and the replacement buildings are nearly all highly mediocre and characterless.

PORTLAND ROAD

Portland Road wasn't in Hove to begin with, but was part of Aldrington, starting life as Clarendon Villas. In 1885, the Aldrington Hotel and a few shops were its only buildings. In 1887 the eastern end was named Bertram Road and the Williamson Homes for Ladies were opened, along with a Wesleyan church. In between were fields, brickfields and market gardens.

In 1892, Hove and Aldrington amalgamated, and four years later the whole stretch of road was named Portland Road, after

the Duke of Portland. By the turn of the century, buildings were virtually continuous on both sides, those between Tamworth Road and the Portland Hotel going up in 1927.

The view here, of the 1930s, shows the Granada Cinema, which opened in 1933. Although titled 'cinema' the Granada was first a theatre, and it seems to have served mixed theatre and cinema use during its early years, but then operated solely as a cinema right up to 1976, when it became the bingo hall it is today (2001 view).

BOUNDARY ROAD

This old view, of about 1900, shows the northern part of Boundary Road, when much of it was still residential. It looks towards the railway crossing and the junction with Portland Road. The early 1960s view, below, was taken further south, with Franklin Road on the left. Many of the old houses remain, but with simple shop fronts added to the ground floors.

The 2001 view shows the street now a jumble of shops, built from the 1960s onwards, with all style and character lost.

The western pavement (left) has been considerably extended. This picture was taken on a Sunday morning, as were most of the Hove views here, and does not show the usual volume of traffic the road has to contend with.

HOVE STREET AND HOVE MANOR

Hove used to consist just of Hove Street and is first pictured on a map of 1545 standing completely on its own, with houses each side and a church to the north. Then it was named Hoove. The population could only have been a few dozen people (even by 1800, the population was only 101). Nothing ancient is left of Hove Street today. The old view, left, of about 1910, looks north. The large building to the left is Hove Cottage, at the corner of Princes Avenue, which was demolished in 1936.

However, the most significant building was Hove Manor House, off to the right, behind the wall where the trees are. This was built about 1790 and is seen in the small view, photographed from Vallance Gardens, when being sold off for demolition in 1936. Hove Corporation could have bought it and used it for some civic purpose, but declined. Historian Antony Dale rated this property the finest individual, secular building in all of Brighton and Hove, second only to the Royal Pavilion. A small section of garden wall, seen below, survived the clearance, but nothing else, and this once historic thoroughfare has become just another street in Hove (2001 view).

KINGSWAY – THE ADUR HOTEL

Our final four pictures take us to the Adur Hotel on Hove's seafront and a grisly story associated with the site. The original inn here dated from 1859 and was run by a Thomas Cordwell. This is seen in the 1930 view, below, before Charringtons took over and rebuilt it in 1931. The smaller view is earlier, 1923, with the hotel standing isolated on a very desolate-looking seafront road.

The rebuilt premises are seen in the mid-1950s view, opposite, below, with the view of 2001 showing the inn extended and now bearing the name Kingsway 330.

The main interest though, is with the cottage that stood here before the first hotel was built. It was occupied by a woman named Rook, whose son, James, was publicly hanged at Goldstone Bottom (the northwest corner of Hove Park today) in

1793, for stealing half a sovereign from a letter carried by a mail rider travelling between Shoreham and Brighton.

Another man, Edward Howell, was also involved, and was hanged with him. The bodies were gibbeted – hung in banded metal frames – and it is

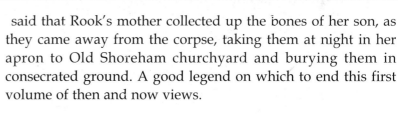

said that Rook's mother collected up the bones of her son, as they came away from the corpse, taking them at night in her apron to Old Shoreham churchyard and burying them in consecrated ground. A good legend on which to end this first volume of then and now views.

ABOUT THE AUTHOR

Chris Horlock was born, brought up and educated in Brighton, living in the town for more than thirty years. In 1976 he emerged from a four-year degree course in teaching at the old Brighton College of Education, at Falmer. His first post was at Glebe Middle School, Southwick, a short distance from where he now lives, and presently he teaches at Thomas a Becket Middle School, Worthing, where he is humanities co-ordinator. He is married with two children, who have an awful lot of pets, several of which share the tiny box-room office where he writes his books.

Future book plans include *Brighton Then and Now, Volume II*, and a short guidebook for visitors to Brighton, *The Neat And Nippy Guide To Brighton*, both to be published in 2002. Also in 2002, the premiere of his play *Magpie's Child* will be staged and he hopes some publisher will take up a children's story he wrote many years ago, *Fingers Five!*